JAZMIN
Saves a Baby Turtle

Copyright © 2022 Rocío Zanca Oubre

All rights reserved.

No part of this publication may be reproduced, stored in a retrieval system, or transmitted in any form or by any means, electronic, mechanical, photocopying, recording, or otherwise, without written permission from the publisher. For information regarding permission, write to Rocío Zanca Oubre.

Published in Spring, Texas.

ISBN:
979-8-2180155-9-6 Hardcover
979-8-9868566-0-5 Paperback
979-82180155-8-9 EPUB

Written and Illustrated by Rocío Zanca Oubre

One day in the summer, Jazmin and Aden played in the yard. Suddenly, Jazmin saw something move that looked like a little rock. It was green and... it had legs! "A baby turtle!," barked Jazmin.

Aden ran to see the little turtle up close. The poor thing looked scared and tired.

The baby turtle cuddled up next to Jazmin right away. It looked happy and less scared. "I will take care of it and protect it," thought Jazmin.

"What is a baby turtle doing so far from the pond?" asked Aden.

"She must be lost," exclaimed Jazmin. They took the little turtle inside the house and put her in a clear box that their mom gave them.

Mom made sure that the baby turtle was not hurt, as she worked in an animal rescue center and knew what to do.

"It just needs to rest to recover its strength. I will make sure to keep her in the right temperature to get comfortable," said Mom.

"Maybe she is hungry," thought Jazmin, "Could the baby turtle eat pizza? What about hot dogs, French fries or ice cream?" asked Jazmin.

"No," Aden responded, "Mom said turtles eat fruits, veggies, insects, worms, and little fish," explained Aden.

Jazmin was very excited to take care of the baby turtle, but she was still confused on how the baby turtle came to her yard. "Could the baby turtle have arrived in a spaceship?" asked Jazmin.

"Could a bird have tried to eat the baby turtle, but then dropped the turtle while flying?"

"Could the baby turtle have gotten lost in the woods?" Jazmin asked. Even though Jazmin could not understand how the turtle arrived, she knew she had to take care of her.

Jazmin thought that the little turtle should have a cute name. "We should name it Lucky," said Aden. "We should name it Peaches," said Jazmin.

"How about you name the baby turtle Lucky Peaches?" said Dad. Aden and Jazmin agreed to the turtle's new name: Lucky Peaches.

Aden decorated the clear box with different shaped rocks; he made a little pool, a little house, and drew the forest on a piece of cardboard so that Lucky Peaches would feel at home. But Lucky Peaches only looked at the forest colored on the cardboard.

Jazmin watched over Lucky Peaches day and night. Lucky Peaches gained her strength and appetite within a few days.

Even though Lucky Peaches was healthier, she seemed to look very sad. Aden and Jazmin noticed Lucky Peaches would spend most of her time looking at the drawing of the forest.

Aden and Jazmin thought maybe Lucky Peaches might be missing being near other turtles. "I think Lucky Peaches would be happier in the pond, with other turtles like her," exclaimed Aden.

Jazmin and Aden decided to take Lucky Peaches to a pond close to their house, where a group of turtles live.

The walk from the house to the pond was very sad for Aden and Jazmin, because they felt like they were losing their little friend.

When Lucky Peaches touched the grass and inhaled the fresh air of the park, her little face was filled with joy. When she wet her feet in the water of the pond, she understood that this was her new home.

After a couple minutes of swimming at the shore, Lucky Peaches decided to explore further out. Once she got farther away from them, she waved in a sign of goodbye. Jazmin and Aden watched Lucky Peaches swim deeper into the pond.

When Aden and Jazmin returned home, they told their dad what happened. "You did the right thing," said Dad, "You should feel proud of yourselves; not only did you save the baby turtle, but you also gave her a name, fed her, took care of her, and lastly found her a new home in the pond. Now she is a happy turtle, and I am sure she will remember you, and you will live in her heart forever."

"Do you think we will see Lucky Peaches again, Dad?" asked Aden.
"We will go to the pond tomorrow, and maybe we will see her," said Dad.

The next morning, Jazmin, Aden, and their dad woke up very early to go to the pond in hopes to see Lucky Peaches.

The three of them took the path to the pond running as fast as they could.

They looked everywhere—between the bushes, over the rocks, and at the grassy edges of the pond—and there she was, on a flat rock at the other shore. Aden and Jazmin ran to say hello.

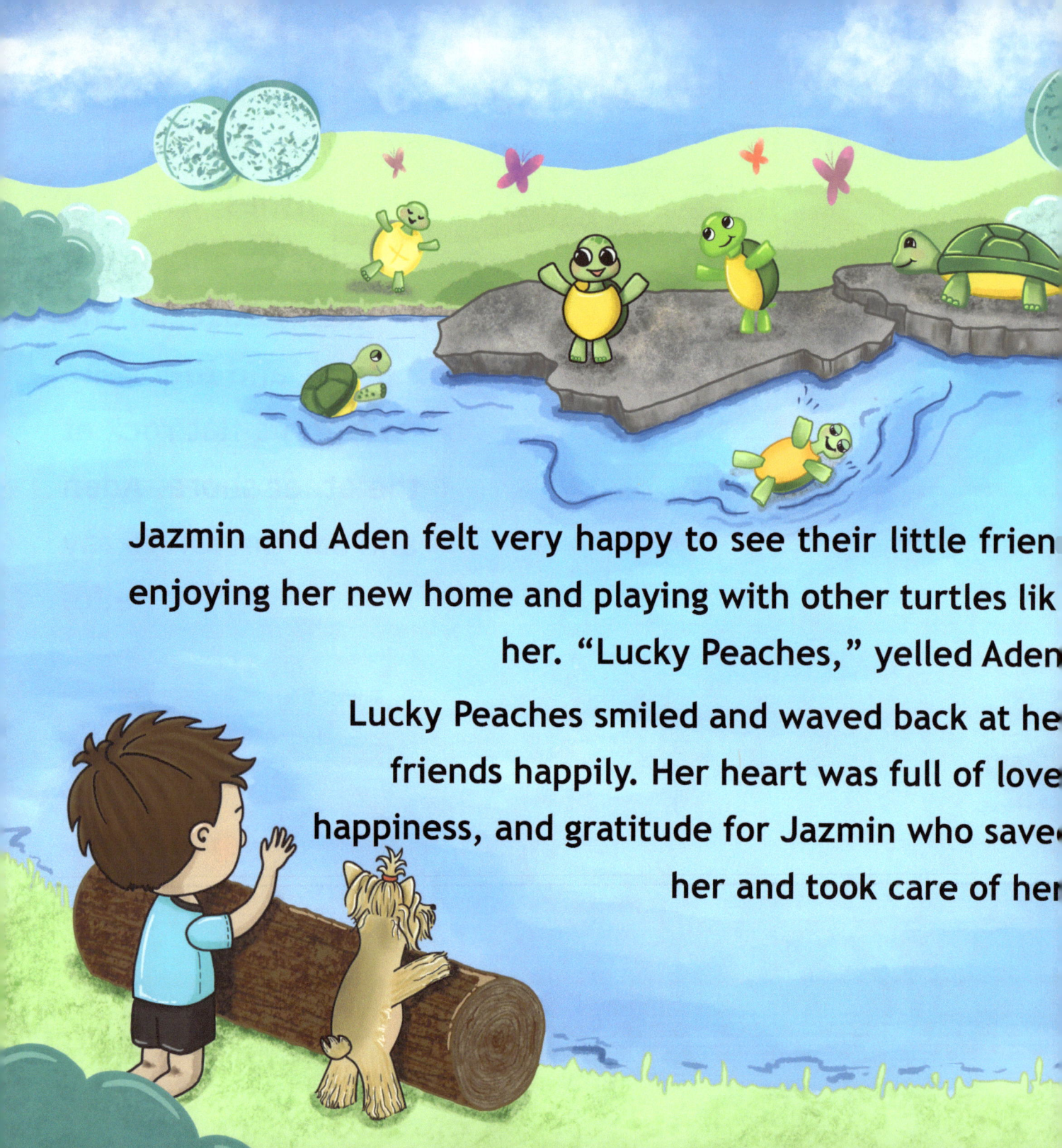

Jazmin and Aden felt very happy to see their little frien[d] enjoying her new home and playing with other turtles lik[e] her. "Lucky Peaches," yelled Aden[.]

Lucky Peaches smiled and waved back at he[r] friends happily. Her heart was full of love[,] happiness, and gratitude for Jazmin who save[d] her and took care of her[.]

Jazmin and Aden would often visit Lucky Peaches at the pond. Jazmin was very proud to have saved Lucky Peaches and the three of them learned that friendship is forever.

About the Author

Rocío Zanca Oubre is a children's book author and illustrator who loves creating stories filled with kindness, courage, and heart. She believes that small acts of love can make a big difference — just like Jazmin does. When she's not writing, she enjoys spending time with her family and dreaming up new adventures.

Follow Jazmin on Instagram at:

https://www.instagram.com/jazmin_the_yorkie/

Follow the Author on Instagram at:

https://www.instagram.com/rocio_zanca_oubre_author/

For Free Printable Colouring Pages, visit the website:

www.rociozancaoubre.com

www.ingramcontent.com/pod-product-compliance
Lightning Source LLC
LaVergne TN
LVHW070434080526
838201LV00132B/268